AFTERNO

for

CRAFTY COOKS

Afternoon Tea for Crafty Cooks

by Diane Ashmore

First published in 2012 by Diane Ashmore

dianeashmore.com

how-to-be-a-bad-artist.com

ISBN: 978-0-9573661-0-7

Written and illustrated by Diane Ashmore

Photography by Diane Ashmore

For more information about the author see page 40.

Thanks to Bert for his advice and the Inspirational Reading Group for their support in this project.

Notes for the Reader
This book uses both metric and imperial measurements. Follow the same units of measurements thoughout. All spoon measurements are level, teaspoons are assumed to be 5ml, and tablespoons are assumed to be 15ml. Unless otherwise stated, milk is full fat and eggs are medium.

Garnishes, decorations and serving suggestions are all optional. Cooking times may vary from those given.

Vegetarians and those with special diets or allergies should check the packaging of ready-made ingredients before use.

CONTENTS

TIME FOR TEA

Afternoon tea is a time for a good gossip and indulgence. You can enjoy it as a birthday celebration, with family, a get-together treat with friends, or as a themed children's party. I've collected tried and trusted recipes and created a few craft projects to give your afternoon tea that personal touch.

Essential ingredients for the best ever afternoon tea:

- Good quality **loose tea leaves**, such as Earl Grey, Darjeeling or Ceylon.
- A **teapot** large enough to make at least two to four cups of tea, no bigger. Use more than one teapot, if necessary, and keep warm with tea cosies.
- **Tea sets**: use tea cups and saucers for a little retro chic. A decorated ceramic teapot or two makes an appealing centrepiece.
- A **cake stand** or tier not only looks pretty, it will also make it easier for your guests to keep an eye on their favourite cake.
- **Cakes and niceties** need to be as pretty and pleasing to the eye as they are to the tastebuds.
- **Good company**: it is essential to invite guests that love to gossip and aren't afraid that a few cakes will "ruin their figure".

"Tea...the cup
that cheers
but not
inebriates"

Mrs Beeton's Book of Household Management

HANDMADE ENVELOPE AND INVITATION

These handmade envelopes, adapted from a traditional origami design, reveal an invitation when you pull the flaps. Who could resist?

You Will Need:

- A4 white paper
- A4 craft paper with a pattern on both sides
- vellum paper
- pen
- ribbon
- decorative stickers
- eyelets and eyelet tool (optional)

1. Try with a piece of A4 white paper first, before using craft paper. Fold one side of the paper by roughly one third of the length. Fold in the other side, so that it is evenly divided into thirds.
2. Fold the two side flaps in half, as shown.
3. Turn the paper over and fold in all four corners of the bottom layer.
4. Turn the paper over again and fold in both sides, as shown.

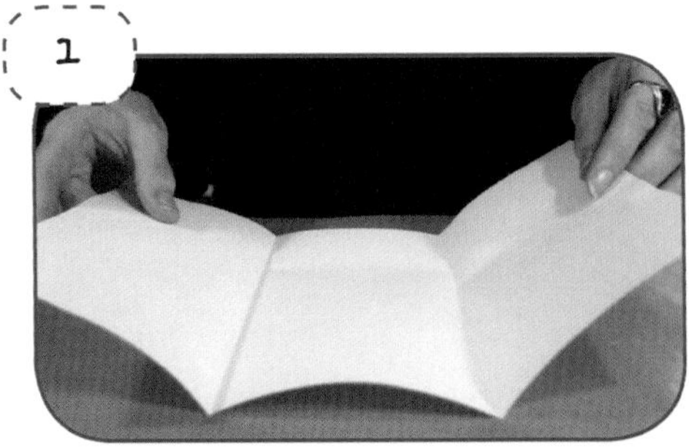

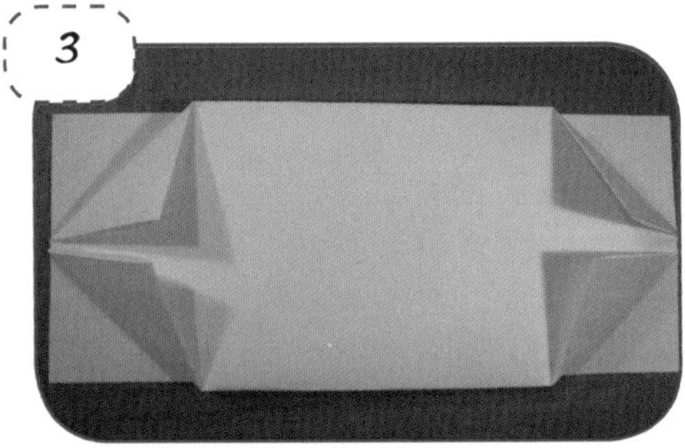

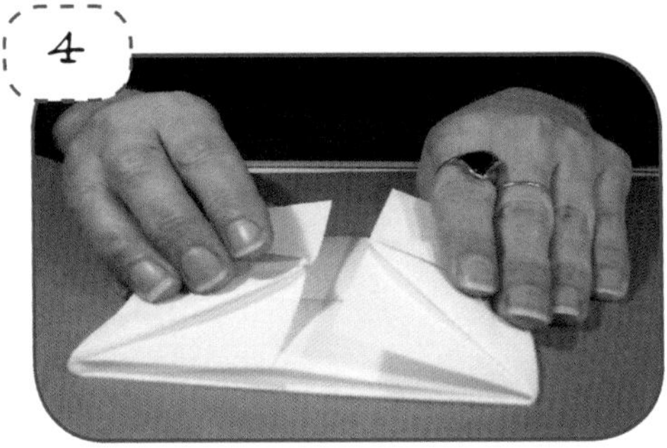

5

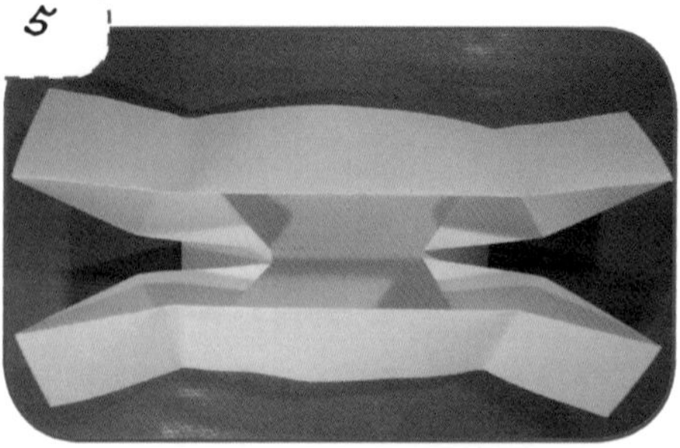

6

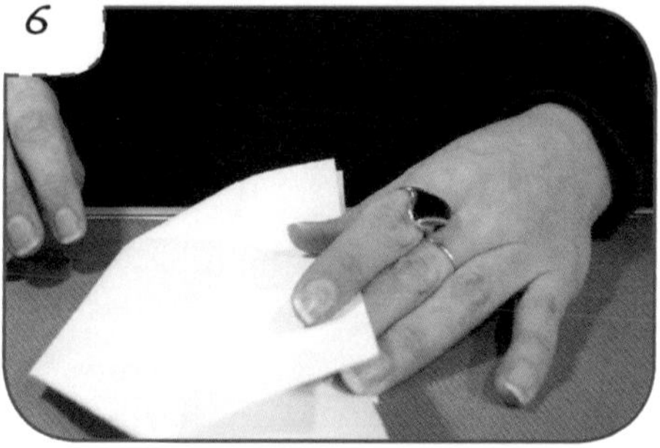

7

8

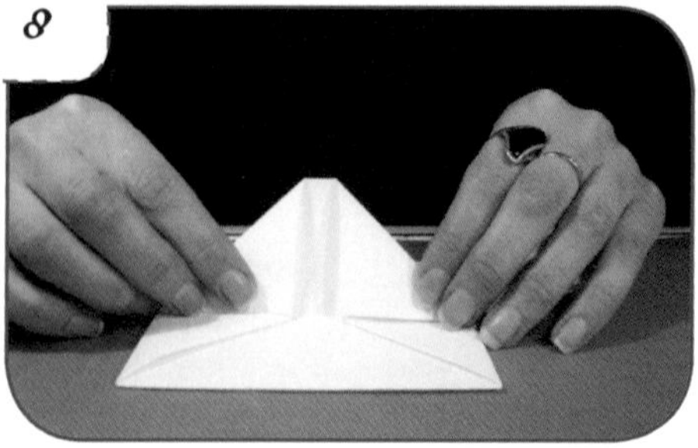

5. Open out the paper and then collapse it again so that it lies flat.
6. With the paper still facing the same way, fold one flap to lie on top of the other.
7. Fold in the two opposite sides of the uppermost flap. Do the same for the flap on the other side.
8. Fold in the two top corners on both sides. You will need to do the same for the other side.

9

10

11

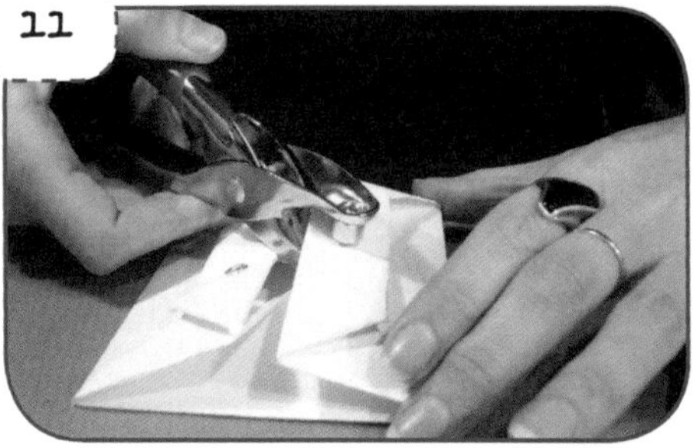

9. Cut the vellum to the correct size to fit the envelope. Write your invitation and insert. Finally, wrap the envelope in ribbon and secure with a sticker.
10. An alternative method of adding ribbon is to fold the flaps in again.

11. Add eyelets to the centre of each flap. Tie a ribbon through the eyelets, to finish.

REVERSIBLE TEA COSY

This tea cosy not only looks great but uses up any scraps of material or old clothes. Turn it inside out for an alternative look.

You Will Need:

- tape measure
- white paper
- black pen
- scissors
- pins
- woollen or fleece material in two colours, such as an old pink sweater and blue fleece top
- wadding material
- tailor's chalk
- felt scraps in various colours
- embroidery threads in various colours
- sewing needle
- beads or buttons
- sewing machine and sewing thread

1. Measure your chosen teapot. The tea cosy will need to be at least 5cm/2 inches wider than the teapot. Draw a semi-circle onto a piece of paper. Cut it out with scissors and use this as a template.

2. Pin the template to your chosen fabric and draw around it with tailor's chalk. Cut two semi-circles in the pink material, two semi-circles in the blue material and two from the wadding.

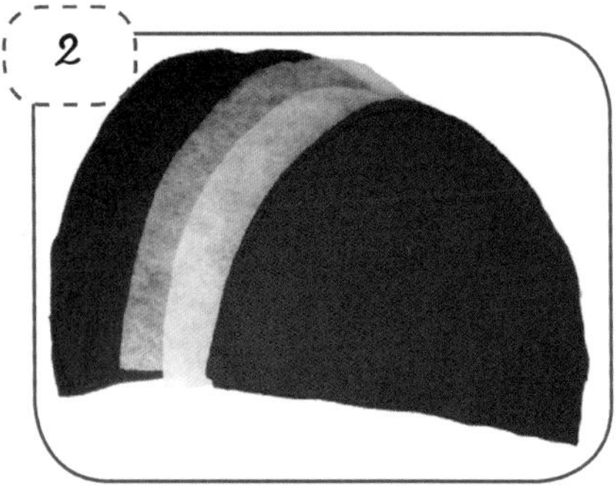

3. Before sewing the pieces together, decorate one of the semi-circles using some of the felt scraps.

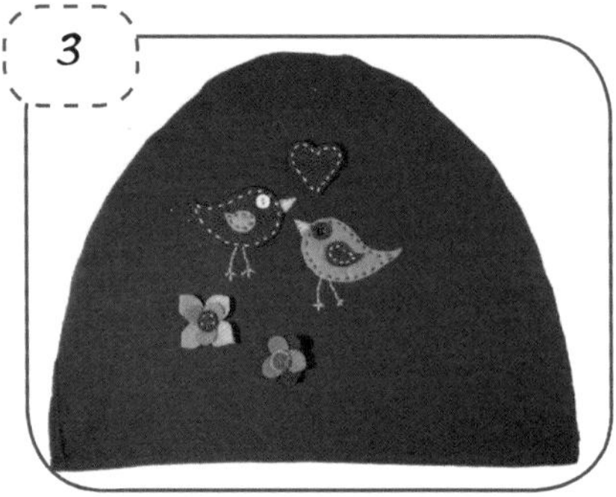

4. Cut out two bird shapes and two wings. Sew them to the semicircle using running stitch. Cut out two triangles for the beaks and stitch them in place. Sew on a button as an eye. Stitch two bird legs with blue embroidery thread.
5. Cut out petal shapes in different colours from the felt scraps. Cut circles in various colours. Stitch them in place using embroidery thread to look like flowers.

6. Cut out hearts from the felt scraps and stitch them in place above the birds.
7. Pin three layers of material together.

Place the pink material on the bottom, the wadding in the middle and the decorated blue material on top. With a sewing machine, stitch a double row of running stitch along the bottom straight edge. Repeat with the other three pieces of material.
8. Pin all the pieces together and sew about 1cm/½ inch from the outer curved edge. Trim the material to the edge of the stitching. Sew another row at least 1cm/½ inch from the first stitch line.
9. To finish, sew a decorative edge, using blanket stitch.

INDIVIDUAL CUPCAKE BOX

At the end of the tea party, it's always nice to give your guests something to take home. This gift box fits one Strawberry Cupcake (see page 32).

You Will Need:

- A4 craft paper with a pattern on both sides
- scissors
- bradawl
- various brads
- hole punch
- ribbon or rope
- paper flowers

1. Take an A4 sheet of craft paper (21 x 28cm/8¼ x 11 inches approximately), and fold one of the shorter edges over by 1cm (½ inch). Then fold in half lengthways. Unfold and fold both shorter sides to the centre crease. Unfold and fold in the longer sides into thirds as shown by the dotted lines.

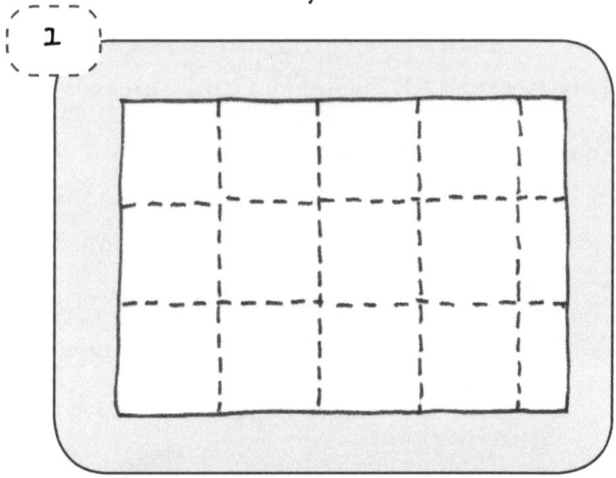

2. Cut out the sides to form a top flap and cut three flaps along the sides, as shown by the straight lines in the diagram, using the folds as a guide.

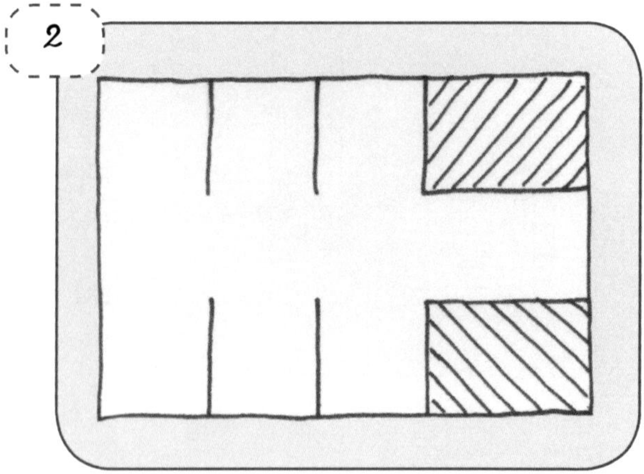

3. Fold the flaps as shown in the diagram. Then fold the sides in to create a box shape. Bring the two triangular flaps together at the sides. With a bradawl, make two holes on each side and secure the flaps in place with two decorative brads.

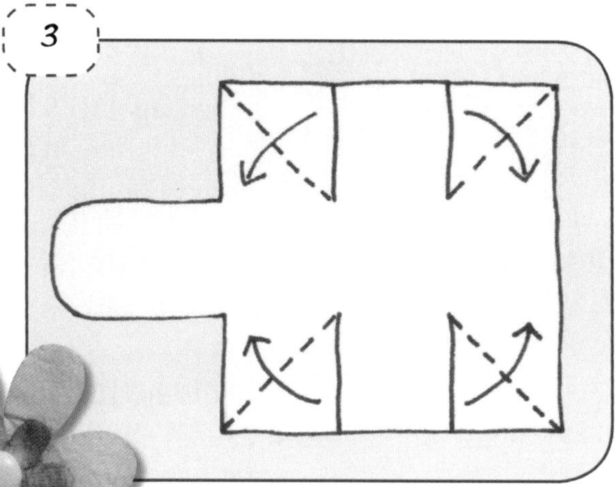

4. Punch holes in the centre of the sides and thread a ribbon through, tying a knot to secure in place. Decorate with a paper flower, secured in place with another brad.

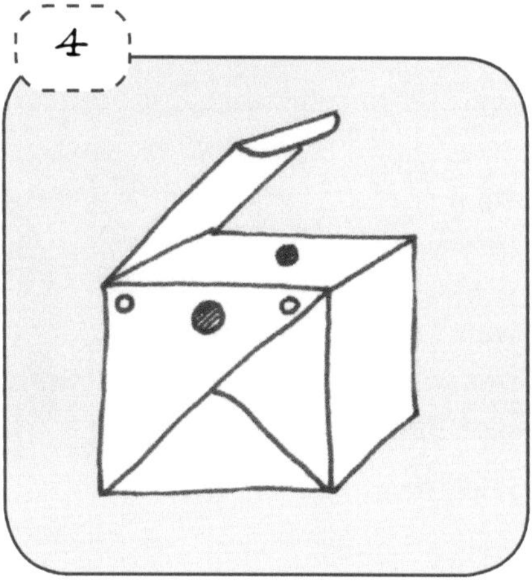

THE PERFECT 'CUPPA' TEA

Make tea with loose tea leaves in a teapot for the best flavour.

Ingredients

- 1 tsp loose tea for each person, plus 1 tsp 'for the teapot'

Method

1. Fill the teapot with boiling water; let it remain for 2 or 3 minutes for the teapot to become warm, then pour the water away. Handle the hot teapot with care.
2. Put in the loose tea, as required, pour in from 300–450ml/ ½–¾ pint of boiling water depending on the size of your teapot, close the lid. Let it stand, for the tea to draw, from 5 to 10 minutes. Stir before filling the teapot up with more boiling water, if necessary.

Hint: Use boiling water. Don't be in a rush to drink the tea as soon as the water fills the pot. Keep the pot warm with a tea cosy (see Reversible Tea Cosy, page 12).

"There is very little art in making good tea; if the water is boiling and there is no sparing of the fragrant leaf, the beverage will almost invariably be good."

Mrs. Beeton's Book of Household Management.

HOMEMADE LEMONADE

On a hot summer's day, it is refreshing to serve lemonade from tall tumblers filled with ice and slices of lemon.

Ingredients

- the rind of 2 lemons
- 225g/8oz sugar, or to taste
- the juice of 3 large or 4 small lemons
- 1.2 litres/2 pints of boiling water
- slices of lemon and ice cubes, to serve

Method

1. Place the lemon rind and sugar to taste in a heatproof jug. Add the lemon juice and pour over the boiling water.
2. When the sugar is dissolved and the water cooled, strain the lemonade through a fine sieve or piece of muslin.
3. Chill in the refrigerator until ready to serve with ice and slices of lemon.

"If life gives you a lemon, make lemonade."

MINI PIZZAS

These are a great alternative to sandwiches and children will love them. You can prepare them beforehand and cook just before it's time to eat.

Ingredients

pizza dough

- 250g/9oz strong white bread flour, plus extra
- 1 tsp of easy-blend dried yeast
- 1 tbsp olive oil
- 125ml/ 4 fl oz of warm water, plus extra

topping

- 8 tsp tomato purée
- 125g/4½oz mozzarella cheese
- 40g/1½oz sliced, pitted olives

Method

1. Sift the flour into a bowl and add the yeast. Pour the oil into the bowl. Add the water gradually to form a soft dough. Use more water if necessary. Knead on a floured surface and return to the bowl and cover with a tea towel. Leave to rise until doubled in size.

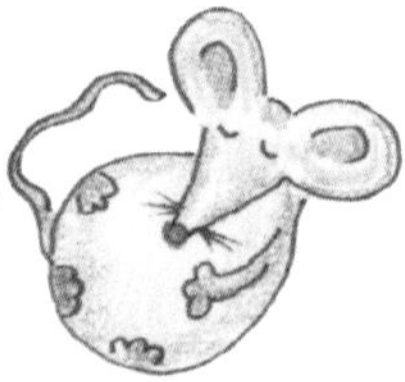

2. Preheat the oven to 200°C/ 400°F /Gas Mark 6. Knead the dough again on a floured surface and roll into eight balls. Roll out the balls to form mini-pizza rounds 5–8cm (2–3¼ inches) in diameter. Add tomato purée, sliced mozzarella cheese and olives, or any topping of your choice.
3. Bake in the preheated oven for 10 minutes or until cooked.

Alternative toppings: Add Feta cheese, onions and sliced fresh tomatoes or tomato purée, mozzarella cheese and sliced chorizo sausage.

Hint: To get the water to the right temperature for adding to the yeast and flour, use one part boiling to two parts cold water and stir.

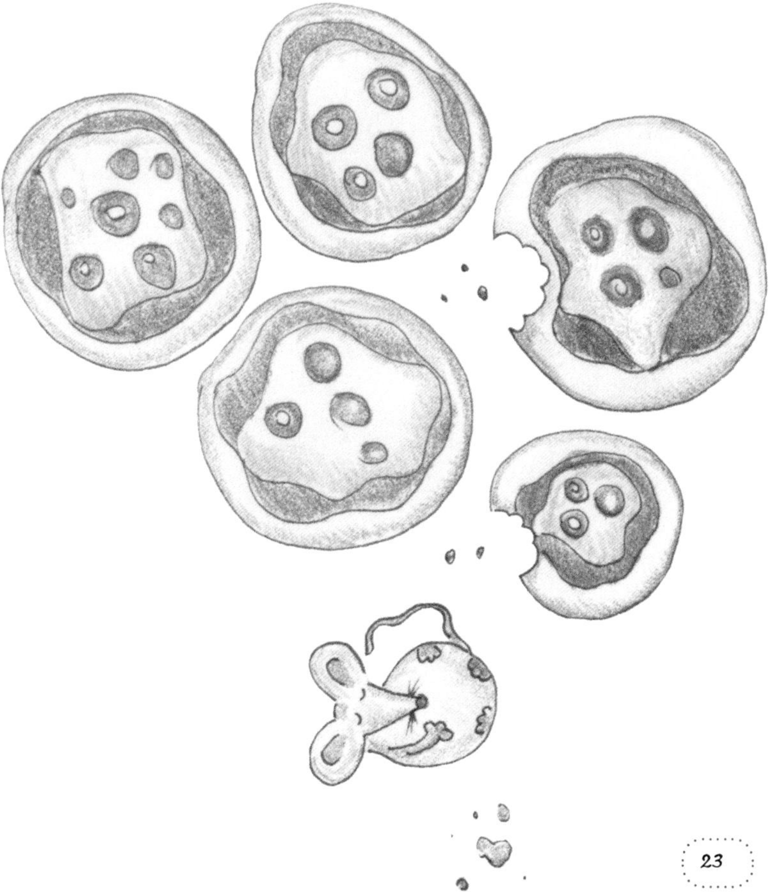

PROPER CUCUMBER SANDWICHES

For a quintessentially English afternoon tea, you cannot go without cucumber sandwiches.

Ingredients

- butter, softened to room temperature
- Soft white bread, thinly sliced

filling

- cucumber, peeled de-seeded and thinly sliced
- salt

Method

1. Butter the bread slices to the edges. Add the cucumber and salt to taste.
2. Place a buttered slice of bread on top and with a sharp knife cut off the crusts.
3. Cut the sandwiches in half and serve with the filling showing at the top.

Alternative sandwich fillings:

Ham and mustard

Use ham, thinly sliced, spread with English mustard or cranberry sauce, to taste.

Egg

Mash hard-boiled eggs and add mayonnaise, to taste.

"The legendary sandwich is thought to be named after the 4th Earl of Sandwich, who asked for roast beef to be brought to him between two slices of toast during a mammoth gambling session."

BERT'S SQUARE SCONES

Bert, a retired professional baker, provided this recipe, which saves time by cutting the scone dough into squares.

Ingredients

- oil, for greasing
- 25g/1 oz fresh yeast, or 7g/¼oz of easy-blend dried yeast
- 450g/1lb plain flour, plus extra for dusting
- 25g/1oz caster sugar, plus extra if required for the yeast
- 2 tsp baking powder
- 115g/4oz unsalted butter, diced
- 250ml/9fl oz milk, plus extra for brushing
- clotted cream and strawberry jam, to serve

Method

1. Grease a baking tray with oil.
2. If using fresh yeast, you will need to activate it. Mix 3 teaspoons boiling water with 3 teaspoons cold water and 1 teaspoon sugar. Mix in the fresh yeast. After a few minutes, the surface should be covered with bubbles.
3. Meanwhile, sift the flour, sugar and baking powder into a bowl. Add the dried yeast at this stage, if not using fresh. Rub in the butter until the mixture resembles fine breadcrumbs. Add the fresh yeast, if using.

Hint: When activating fresh yeast, the water needs to be warm but not too hot as this will kill the yeast. Salt will also kill fresh yeast.

4. Pour in enough milk to make a soft dough, but do not over knead the dough.
5. Roll out the scones on a lightly flour surface to about 1cm/½ inch thick. Cut the dough into squares. Preheat the oven to 220°C/425°F/Gas Mark 7. Leave to rise for 30 minutes. Brush the tops with milk. Bake in the preheated oven for 10–12 minutes until well risen.
6. Serve with clotted cream and strawberry jam.

Variation: Add 115g/4oz of sultanas in step 4 to make fruit scones.

EARL GREY TEA LOAF

Sultanas soaked in tea add a great flavour to this tasty tea loaf.

Ingredients

- 2 tsp loose Earl Grey tea or 1 Earl Grey teabag
- 225g/8oz sultanas
- 450g/1lb strong white bread flour, plus extra for dusting
- pinch of salt
- 2 tsp mixed spice
- 115g/4oz caster sugar
- 25g/1oz fresh yeast, or 7g/¼oz of easy-blend dried yeast
- 115g/4oz unsalted butter, diced
- 150ml/5fl oz milk
- 1 egg
- oil, for greasing

Method

1. Boil enough water to fill a teapot or jug and add the Earl Grey tea. Leave to brew for a few minutes. Place the sultanas in a bowl and pour the tea over. Leave to soak for at least half an hour.
2. Sift the flour, salt, mixed spice, sugar and yeast into a bowl and rub in the butter until the mixture resembles fine breadcrumbs.
3. Warm the milk and beat the egg before adding to the flour mixture. Add the soaked sultanas. Knead the dough on a lightly floured surface and return to the bowl to rise for 2 hours.

4. Preheat the oven to 180°C/350°F/Gas Mark 4 and grease a 900-g/2-lb loaf tin. Knead the dough again, then place in the prepared tin and leave to rise for 20 minutes. Bake in the preheated oven for 1 hour 10 minutes or until golden and well risen. Leave to cool before serving.

Hint: You can buy fresh yeast from most supermarkets with a fresh bakery in store. If you cannot locate fresh yeast use easy-blend dried yeast instead.

CHERRY SHORTBREAD

Add glacé cherries to make a delicious short-bread with this really easy recipe.

Ingredients

- 300 g/10 ½ oz plain flour, plus extra for dusting
- 85 g/3 oz cornflour
- 115 g/4 oz unsalted butter, plus extra for greasing
- 115 g/4 oz margarine
- 115 g/4 oz caster sugar
- 1 tsp vanilla essence
- 115 g/4 oz glacé cherries, chopped, plus halves to decorate

Method

1. Preheat the oven to 180°C/ 350°F/ Gas Mark 4. Lightly grease two baking sheets. Sift together the flour and cornflour and set aside.
2. Soften the butter and margarine in a bowl and beat in the sugar with a wooden spoon. Add the vanilla essence. Gradually add the flour mixture and mix to a soft dough. Add the chopped glacé cherries.

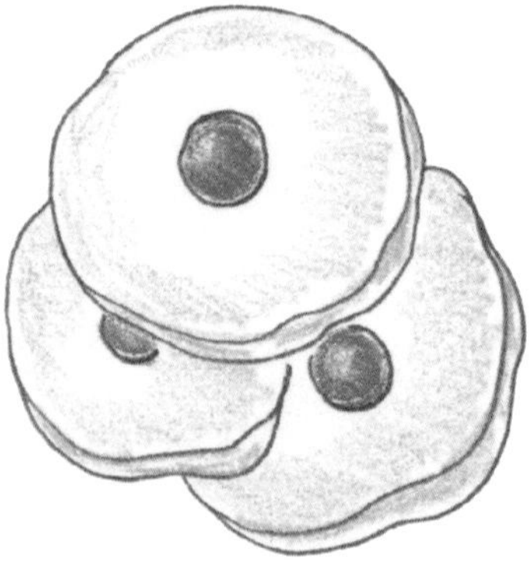

Hint: Freeze the dough for up to a month. Defrost and cook as per the recipe.

3. Roll out the dough on a lightly floured surface to a thickness of 1cm/½ inch. Using a round dough cutter, cut out rounds of dough, re-rolling until all the dough is used up.
4. Press glacé cherry halves on top of the rounds. Place the rounds on the prepared baking sheets and bake in the preheated oven for 15–20 minutes. Leave to cool on a wire rack before serving.

STRAWBERRY CUPCAKES

A very easy recipe that looks luscious with fresh strawberries perched on top.

Ingredients

- 115g /4 oz butter, plus extra for greasing
- 115g /4 oz caster sugar
- 2 large eggs
- 115g /4 oz self raising flour
- 1 tbsp cocoa powder
- 1 tsp vanilla essence
- pinch of salt

Topping

- 100g/3½oz strawberry flavour chocolate buttons
- 100g/3½oz thick Greek-style yogurt
- halved fresh strawberries, to decorate

Method

1. Preheat the oven to 220°C /425°F /Gas Mark 7. Cream the butter with the sugar and stir in the eggs. Sift in the flour and cocoa, add the vanilla essence, a pinch of salt and stir. Place bun cases in greased bun tins and half fill them. Cook for 15–20 minutes in the preheated oven, before removing to cool on a wire rack.
2. Make the topping. Melt the strawberry flavour chocolate in a heatproof bowl over simmering water. Remove from the heat and mix in the yogurt. Spread on top of the cupcakes with a spoon and add half a strawberry to decorate.

BRANDYLESS SNAPS

This is a tricky recipe to get right, but fun to try. Take care as the snaps get very hot once they leave the oven.

Ingredients

- 50g/ 1¾oz light brown sugar
- 50g/ 1¾oz butter
- 2 tbsp golden syrup
- 50g/1¾oz plain flour
- ½tsp ground ginger
- ½tsp vanilla essence
- oil, for greasing
- whipped cream, to serve

Method

1. Preheat the oven to 180°C/ 350°F/ Gas Mark 4. Mix the sugar, butter, and golden syrup together in a saucepan and heat at a very low temperature until the sugar is melted. Remove from the heat before the sugar crystallizes. Stir in the flour, ginger and vanilla to form a soft dough.
2. Using two teaspoons, shape the dough into small round blobs. Bake four at a time on a baking sheet in the preheated oven for 10 minutes. Remove from the oven and leave to cool for a few moments. Shape around an oiled handle of a wooden spoon, taking care as it will be very hot. Leave to cool before filling with whipped cream using a piping bag.

Hint: If the biscuit becomes too hard to curl, return to the oven until warm.

GINGERBREAD WOMEN

You can shape gingerbread into any form that you choose. Why settle for gingerbread men?

Ingredients

- 350g/12 oz plain flour, plus extra for dusting
- 1 tsp baking powder
- 1 tsp ground ginger
- 1 tsp mixed spice
- 175g/6oz light soft brown sugar
- 55g/2oz butter, plus extra for greasing
- 55g/2oz margarine
- 1 large egg
- 4 tbsp golden syrup
- 2 tbsp milk (optional)
- raisins and chopped glacé cherries, to decorate

Method

1. Sift the flour, baking powder, ginger, mixed spice and sugar into a bowl. Add the butter and margarine and blend until the mixture resembles fine breadcrumbs.
2. Lightly beat the egg and stir in the golden syrup. Add milk, if necessary, to make a soft dough. Knead on a floured surface before covering in cling film and chilling in the refrigerator for 15 minutes.
3. Preheat the oven to 180°C/ 350°F/ Gas Mark 4. Grease two baking sheets.
4. Roll out the dough to about 1cm/ ½ inch thick on a floured surface. To make women, cut out a gingerbread man with a cookie cutter and add a triangle

on top to form a skirt. Add raisins for eyes and buttons and glacé cherries for lips.

5. Place on the baking sheets leaving gaps and cook in the preheated oven for 10–15 minutes, or until light golden brown. Leave on the tray for 10 minutes before transferring to a wire rack to cool.

Hint: Make shoes and handbags using coloured icing for extra fun.

PINK CHOCOLATE MICE

Chocolate mice are so quick and easy to make. You can buy silicone mice moulds from a good cookware store.

Ingredients

- 200g/7oz pink strawberry flavour buttons

Method

1. Place the pink chocolate buttons in a heatproof bowl.
2. Melt the chocolate buttons in a heatproof bowl over a pan of simmering water.
3. Pour into silicone mouse moulds.
4. Cool in the refrigerator until hardened. Remove from the moulds and serve.

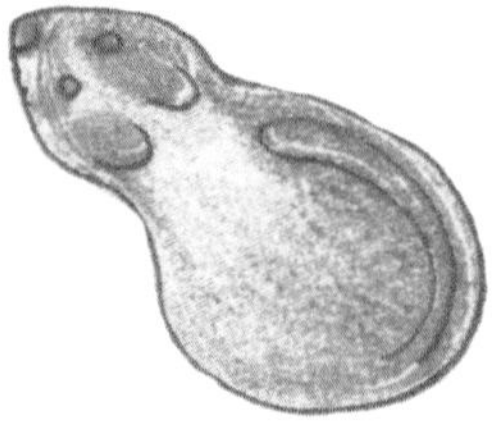

Alternative: Use milk or white chocolate buttons instead of the pink strawberry ones to create chocolate mice in different colours.

INDEX

ABOUT THE AUTHOR

Diane Ashmore is a writer, artist and editor, who lives in Cambridgeshire.

She loves to share her arts and crafts projects with others on how-to-be-a-bad-artist.com. You can see a portfolio of her work on her blog dianeashmore.com.

She contributes to craft magazines and is a keen, self-taught, amateur cook.